Haiku Forest Afterlife

Robert Epstein

Middle Island Press

2014

Haiku Forest Afterlife

ISBN 978-0-6922-2170-9

"Snow Moon" Cover Art by Ron C. Moss; used by permission

www.ronmoss.com

Published by Middle Island Press
PO Box 354
West Union WV 26456

Because I could not stop for death/He kindly stopped for me;/ The carriage held but just ourselves/And Immortality.

~ *Emily Dickinson*

It is the secret of the world that all things subsist and do not die, but only retire a little from sight and afterwards return again.

~ *Ralph Waldo Emerson*

I look upon death to be as necessary to the constitution as sleep. We shall rise refreshed in the morning.

~ *Benjamin Franklin*

As long as you are not aware of the continual law of Die and Be Again, you are merely a vague guest on a dark Earth.

~ *Johann Wolfgang von Goethe*

If you stay in the center/and embrace death with your whole heart/ you will endure forever.

~ Lao Tzu

Death is nothing else but going home to God, the bond of love will be unbroken for eternity.

~ *Mother Teresa*

Live so that thou mayest desire to live again--that is thy duty--for in any case thou wilt live again!

~ *Friedrich Nietzsche*

The soul takes nothing with her to the next world but her education and her culture.

~ *Plato*

After your death, you will be what you were before your birth.

~ *Arthur Schopenhauer*

The day which we fear as our last is but the birth of eternity.

~ *Seneca*

I am confident that there truly is such a thing as living again, that the living spring from the dead, and that the souls of the dead are in existence.

~ *Socrates*

It is not more surprising to be born twice than once; everything in nature is resurrection.

~ *Voltaire*

The real question of life after death isn't whether or not it exists, but even if it does what problem this really solves.

~ *Ludwig Wittgenstein*

Contents

On Turning Sixty

&

In Honor of:

J. Krishnamurti

Acknowledgments

First and foremost, I want to thank my dear friend, Sophie Soltani, for sharing her unwavering faith in the afterlife. Without in any way being overbearing or dogmatic, she has simply restated her conviction over our twenty year friendship. I am finally willing to peek behind the curtain of uncertainty to at least *sense* what's there, if anything. I also want to express my appreciation to friends and family for their love and support, including Jay Schlesinger and Miriam Wald with whom I have had many conversations about the *big questions*.

I am particularly grateful to fellow haiku poet, Bruce England, who encouraged me to investigate this "last frontier" (to use the words of J. Assante) of haiku. I owe a great debt of gratitude to Roberta Beary as well as Marian Olson, both of whom read the manuscript and offered constructive feedback. Philip Boatright has been a steadfast haiku friend.

I want to thank editors Francine Banwarth and Michele Root-Bernstein for publishing "trade winds" in the haiku journal, *Frogpond*.

My partner and fellow traveler, Stacy Taylor, deserves special thanks for her continuing support of my haiku travels.

Preface

Death is not the end.

~ Bob Dylan

For the longest time I have steadfastly maintained that it is not possible to say a word about what happens after death. Anything that can be said about death is, by definition, expressed by someone *living*. Only the dead can speak with authority about death and the afterlife.

On the other hand, the late haiku poet, Susan Marie LaVallee, who died of cancer, had the courage to write about the afterlife; her poem serves as something of an inspiration to me:

one bead at a time
counting
on an afterlife*

At sixty, I am willing to stretch a bit with regard to the not-knowing stance I have taken for many years. I credit this increased openness to my dear friend, Sophie, who has insisted for more than twenty years that there is *most certainly* life after death. She even maintains, with tongue-in-cheek, that life is way worse than any hell we might subsequently encounter. "The afterlife *has to be* better than this," she has said wryly and on more than one occasion.

Is it possible to inquire into death without the long arm of fear? I took up this challenge which the secular teacher, J. Krishnamurti, poses in *On Living and Dying*:

> . . . [C]an one look at death totally?--which is to have no fear. It is fear with its will to escape that has created all these myths, symbols, beliefs. If you can look at it totally, with your whole being, then you will see that death has a quite different meaning because there is no fear. It is fear that makes us demand to know if there is continuity after death, and fear finds its own response in the belief that there *is* or that there is *not*.
> p. 104

I have been guided over the past thirty-five years or more by Lao Tzu, the ancient Chinese sage and author of *The Tao te Ching.*** Lao Tzu was perfectly comfortable with the ineffable, unknowable, mystery of the Tao --the Way of Nature. I draw inspiration from the Taoist sage's view of life-and-death in relation to the Tao:

> The Tao is infinite, eternal.
> Why is it eternal?
> It was never born;
> thus it can never die.

Susanna, a haiku friend, recently expressed this wish to me: "I hope when you get to heaven at 105, you wake up in a haiku forest." The poems in this collection reflect my exploration of this haiku forest without--to my surprise--the intrusion of much fear. I let my imagination wander out ahead. I make no claim to personal or direct experience of the afterlife. If there is one, I will do my best to make this known to the living, after I die, insofar as I can. Until then, these provisional haiku are what I offer by way of *possibility*. They may prove to be unnecessary.

pen & pad

in my shirt pocket

burial notes

Notes

* *Frogpond*, 32:1, 2009

** *Tao te Ching*. S. Mitchell, tr. New York: Harper & Row, 1988.

Robert Epstein
El Cerrito, CA
8 April 2014

The smallest sprouts show there is really no death,
And if ever there was it led forward life, and does not
wait at the end to arrest it,
And ceased the moment life appeared.
All goes onward and outward... and nothing collapses,
And to die is different from what any one supposed, and
Luckier.

~ Walt Whitman, "Song of Myself," Leaves of Grass

haiku

forest

afterlife

dark wood

w/o Dante I can tell

I'm in *trouble*

near the pine foreshadowing

inspired by roseliep

purchased a pine box

used it for filing till...

~ *for Father Raymond Roseliep* (1)

maple keys

something in me still

wants to grow

obla di obla da

life goes on

till it doesn't

dead

end

the

way

it

slows

you

down

60th

is it time to start

looking for a plot

hospice

every breath

an eternity

comes a time

when the corpse pose

no longer is

last

snowfall

you

can’t

hear

see

or

taste

it

where do we go

when we die, uncle rob

right here

Avalon sunset

catching a glimpse of

more than my self

~ after Van Morrison

candle

smoke

disappears

i

know

where

i

am

going

waking up

death is not

the end

paper trail

at the end of it

my cicada shell

how do i pine box

let me

count the ways

earth element [x]

water element [x]

fire element [x]

wind element [x]

roger, out

6 feet under

the average

zero

that bald head

finally replaced

trimmed grass

new moon

the wish to be

born again

not more than

60 years in the making

this afterlife

reincarnation

how easily the undertaker

breaks it down

white

light

could

be

jesus

or

kerouac

on

the

road (2)

in breath

out breath

no breath

trade winds
figuring out the odds
of an afterlife

psychic prediction

a picture perfect

afterlife

looking back

what were you

a breathing reed

zen garden

nothing could already

be me

on stand-by

at the Pearly Gates

hoping to get lucky

i am dead

& buried but not

the crocus

graveyard

a free spirit

joins the rest

koi pond

a posthumous medium

i could thrive in

Grand Canyon *echoing*

could it be so

the afterlife

a pearl

paradise lost

possibly regained

posthumously

old diary

page after page

the afterlife

post-death moss about covers it

broken compass

starts working again

afterlife

campfire

my afterlife

crackles

pissed off & ready to burn postmortem

fire in the belly of the afterlife

last exit

on the afterlife bullet train

nirvana

not you again!

drunk uncle

afterlife

through the crosshairs

two angels debating

the right to bear arms

afterlife

i inquire about

custom tailoring

dust motes find your place

ball

no

chain

after

life

a name

in melting snow

me, not me

billowing that's who you are now

after death *nothing* to mourn

former criminals

forge guns into lamps

haiku heaven

afterlife

where

the

hell

are

my

keys

d**us**t

~ after Cor van den Heuvel

unbuttoned

all

the

way

down

to

bone

hell or heaven

who cares, just take me

to haiku forest afterlife

blue rain in the haiku forest afterlife

15 gnomes

in three short rows

haiku heaven

the computer screen goes *blank*

afterlife

Puff the Magic Dragon

for real

seagulls glide

on syllables, not wings

haiku heaven

ah, yes! the pathless path of the butterfly

remember those

three day fasts?

it just keeps goin'

nothing of me left to be *contained*

what possums know about the posthumous life

w/o a back it's no longer *bad*

can you *hear* me seashell

leader of the posthumous pack

resurrection sky

there never was anything

to *conquer*

~ *for Roberta Beary*

the afterlife reassembly line

crows sowing seeds afterlife

in no time

circling a new blue moon

in my own way

~ *after Alan Watts*

moonrise

the morning of

your rebirth

rototilling

the night sky

for new spirit

new year's day

dropping in the bucket

of eternity

c

o

m

p

o

s

t

m

e

t

o

o

the call i put off

the amends i meant to make

never happened

air

clouds

sun

water

earth

you

now

you are no-boundary

no

cell

phone

service

that’s

the

afterlife

deep in the backwoods

of the afterlife

Thoreau's hound & bay horse (3)

there never were

four seasons

afterlife

giving me pause

the afterlife

of big lies

my remains

the distant future

of permaculture (4)

wheeling nothing

in the baby carriage

afterlife

finding out

what happens to *sorry*

the afterlife

white space

could be

posthumous poetry

the other meaning

of killing time

after death

afterlife

nothing gained

nothing missed

ants

worms

maggots

rule

high tide

a new armada of

ghosts ride in

won't get fooled

again

afterlife

on second thought

there is none

afterlife

trying to converse
with a cherub, it points
an arrow at me

who rests in peace

soul : man

1

billion

days

here

i

am

again

snow-

man

on the posthumous road again

~ *after Jack Kerouac*

save the date

what for

what if

enlightenment resting in peace

edge of night

coming and going

through the cracks

that

ball

still

floating

still

no

chain

that alien

was me a million

years from now

shattered

light

coming

through

again

upside

down

hour

glass

born

again

here

i

am

a

rain

drop

falling

forever

with

you

Watercourse Way keep going (5)

afterlife?

out of time

dogs run free

I depart as air, I shake my white locks at the runaway sun,
I effuse my flesh in eddies, and drift it in lacy jags.

I bequeath myself to the dirt to grow from the grass I love,
If you want me again look for me under your boot-soles.

You will hardly know who I am or what I mean,
But I shall be good health to you nevertheless,
And filter and fibre your blood.

Failing to fetch me at first keep encouraged,
Missing me one place search another,
I stop somewhere waiting for you.

~ Walt Whitman, "Song of Myself," Leaves of Grass

Notes

1. Father Raymond Roseliep. According to Edward Reilly, "Raymond Roseliep, I believe, did not fear death. He had prepared for it, purchasing a simple wooden coffin that he kept in his apartment, using it as a temporary repository for his manuscripts and other important items." Edward J. Reilly, "Raymond Roseliep Thirty Years Later." *bottle rockets*, #30, 2014, pp. 86-89.

2. Jack Kerouac, the Beat poet in the 50s and 60s who wrote *On the Road* and *Dharma Bums* as well as other Buddhist-inspired writings.

3. Thoreau's hound and bay horse refers to a parable in Henry D. Thoreau's, *Walden*: "I long ago lost a hound, a bay horse, and a turtle-dove and am still on their trail. Many are the travellers I have spoken concerning them, describing their tracks and what calls they answered to. I have met one or two who have heard the hound, and the tramp of the horse, and even seen the dove disappear behind a cloud, and they seemed as anxious to recover them as if they had lost them themselves." In *Walden: The Writings of Henry David Thoreau*. Boston: Houghton-Mifflin, 1906; p. 18-19.

4. Permaculture is the development of agricultural ecosystems that are sustainable and self-sufficient.
5. In the ancient Chinese philosophy of Taoism (pronounced **Dow**ism), the absolute principle underlying the universe, combining within itself the principles of yin and yang and signifying a way of life that is wholly in harmony with the natural order.

Suggested Reading

Archangel, D. *Afterlife Encounters: Ordinary People, Extraordinary Experiences*. Charlottesville, VA: Hampton Roads, 2005.

Assante, J. *The Last Frontier: Exploring the Afterlife and Transforming Our Fear of Death*. Novato, CA: New World Library, 2012.

Chopra, D. *Life After Death: The Burden of Proof*. New York: Harmony Books, 2006.

Krishnamurti, J. *On Living and Dying*. Sandpoint, ID: Morning Light Press, 2004.

Lester, D. *Is There Life After Death? An Examination of the Empirical Evidence*. Jefferson, NC: McFarland, 2005.

Levine, S. *A Year to Live*. New York: Bell Tower, 1997.

________. *Healing into Life and Death*. New York: Anchor, 1989.

________. *Who Dies? An Investigation into Conscious Living and Conscious Dying*. New York: Anchor, 1989.

Lief, J. L. *Making Friends with Death: A Buddhist Guide to Encountering Mortality.* Boston, MA: Shambhala, 2001.

Moody, R. *Reunions: Visionary Encounters with Departed Loved Ones*. New York: Ivy

Ring, K. and Valarino, E. *Lessons from the Light*. Needham, MA: Moment Point Press, 2006.

Rosenberg, L. with Guy, D. *Living in the Light of Death: On the Art of Being Fully Alive*. Boston: Shambhala, 2000.

Sogyal Rinpoche, *The Tibetan Book of Living and Dying*. Gafney, P. and Harvey, A., eds. San Francisco: HarperSanFrancisco, 1994.